KICK A!

How to Ditch Your Type A Personality and
Live a Life You Might Actually ENJOY!

For Ann, Anne, Erin, Estelle, Stephanie, my sister Karen and all of my dear friends who love me always and humor me when necessary.

Special thanks to the staff at the Hyatt Summerfield Suites® Lincoln Park in Dallas, TX. Couldn't have done it without y'all.

The Type A Personality

"... ambitious, aggressive, business-like, controlling, highly competitive, impatient, preoccupied with his or her status, time-conscious, and tightly-wound. People with Type A personalities are often high-achieving "workaholics" who multi-task, push themselves with deadlines, and hate both delays and ambivalence."

Wikipedia

The Type C Personality

"None of the above!"

Inventapedia

There's no A in FREEDOM, but there's a big ole honkin' C in CHOICE!

YOU can Be the C!!!! Let the healing begin!

C is Not Average, Silly, It's BALANCE!

Studies show that Type A personalities are more prone to depression, anxiety, heart attacks, strokes, bad hands at poker, shorter life spans, and a variety of other not so nice medical and mental health maladies. Type C, a life lived in joy-filled balance, gets absolutely no bad press at all! Imagine that!

If I were still a card-carrying member of Type A, I'd tell myself I needed a Masters degree or a doctorate to write this book. I would have had to find an agent or a publisher who was Type A enough to believe I needed a Masters or a PhD to write this book.

Instead, I'm choosing to remember the bottomless pit of hard knocks, cold sweats, 15-round bouts of insomnia, anxiety attacks, feelings of failure, need to compare myself with everyone around me (including house pets) and all of the other nasty bits I experienced as a member in never good enough for me standing of the Sacred Society of Type A (SSTA).

Four years ago, at the tender age of 42, I was at the tippy top of my chosen profession. The lead creative at a marketing agency, I was an Atlas with boobs, holding the orbiting creative worlds of a host of blue chip corporations precariously over my head as I attempted to convince anyone who would listen in every nanosecond of every day that I was the Type A who could lead the way to Nike! (victory, of course, not shoes).

I had to devise ways to prove my worthiness, in every nanosecond of every moment of every day (and often when I was fast or at least uncomfortably asleep), so as not lose my corner office suite to the gaggle of other Type As climbing my corporate ladder. Oh, the PRESSURE. My Type C psyche gets upset just at the memory of it all!

But a funny thing happened on my way once I reached the holy grail of the corner office. I instantly realized something that brought my A to its knees: IT WAS EMPTY! And not in the literal sense of course, as the interior design had been executed and the coffee tables, desk, chairs and couch put in their rightful places. Instead, it was completely and utterly devoid of *meaning* for me! There were no angels singing on high, no magical feeling of discovering the meaning of (corporate) life. Wow! Certainly, this was no way for a Type A to react.

I eventually retreated into forced unemployment, and began to the epic search for new meaning in my life. What was the next mountain I needed to climb? The next achievement I could set my sights on? I asked those questions and more, over and over again, without even a hint (for the first time in my life) what I was supposed to do.

At 42, could my life be OVER? No, my friends! After intensive therapy, soul searching, incessant playing of *The Carpenters Greatest Hits* and long walks in the rain, I realized my life had just begun! The Type C life was emerging in me, and I welcomed its pressure free melody! The vice like grip Type A had on my psyche was dissipating, and I was terrified and thrilled simultaneously!!! Say AMEN!

Ah, but the Type A force is *STRONG.*

If you, even for a second, doubt the power of the Type A movement, try this experiment: Visit a Type Aer at the top of his/her game who has won the corner office. It's a cherished position because (like the Type A bastion of airline first class) you get more (ego driven) head and legroom and usually a bitchin' view.

Look closely. What direction does your Type A friend's desk face? Yep -- the door! Type Aers learn early that to keep your competitive, over achieving corporate position, you must hypervigilently watch your back. Never lose control of your circumstance, and NEVER look at the view. That would be dangerous AND a waste of precious time!

And oh, how simple life would be if we reserved our Type A just for corporate America. Instead, from playgrounds to tricked out birthday parties with Pin the Tail on the politically correct object (you might have once know it as the "donkey"), Type A is the biggest epidemic in the United States today.

3rd world countries that we've looked down on from our long noses of superiority typically have less divorce, anxiety, depression and oodles of other less than nice things that we have in the bucket loads. Those folks are just thinking about how to find joy in their lives outside of everyday trials and tribulations. Their kids don't know how many AP classes at age 5 they'll need to ace to get into Harvard (or what an AP class is or what Harvard is for that matter).

In our Type A world, we've gone from keeping up with the Jones to beating them to a pulp. And friends, it just doesn't give us a golden ticket to Camp Happy – it simply speeds up our race to the end of our journey.

Your years as chairman of the Junior League or Cattle Baron's Ball or all of the other great things you amass can't come with you. No, my friends! Running from achievement to achievement won't make life one second longer. And I suggest it makes your life go a whole lot faster. Who the Sam Heck would want THAT?

The simple fact is that we don't need to build a better muffin than Betsy at the bake sale to live whole, enriched and authentic lives. We can practice the fine art of life living rather than torturing ourselves, gassing up the minivan to run to the 3rd book club of the week and it's only Tuesday. We don't need to multi-task, find more hours in the day or somehow prove ourselves to the Universe. The Universe already digs us!

In order to succeed as a Type C, you must grasp the major misconception of the Type A: Giving 110% is IMPOSSIBLE. Common sense will tell you it doesn't exist. Being an "overachiever" is IMPOSSIBLE. "Achieve" is like "yes" or "no", you either do or you don't so you can't "over". (The only acceptable "overs" for a C would be something like "Oops, I overslept. Must have needed the rest!")

When my old Type A was not at the office, on a plane or in a strange hotel room (note: hotel rooms are all strange, as they're not your house), I ran marathons. The first poor bastard to run a marathon, Philipedes, died after running to the town of Marathon, Greece and announcing the good guys had one the war. Leave it to the Type As to take something that killed the first guy to try it and turn it into a sport you could compete over. What, a warning from God? Pshaw! It was an invitation!!!

The Type C non- theoretic, non-matrixed, non-pie charted process (Type Aers, holler back!) uses the logical part of the Type A brain to rewire itself. Type Aers can learn new tricks. You can learn to live again, without fear of people years from now dancing on your grave, saying what a complete failure you were.

Hearses do not pull u-Hauls.

There is not a single shred of evidence that you can take any of your material possessions, including bank accounts, yachts, org charts with your name at the top, gold stars, blue ribbons, shiny awards or anything else to the hereafter. Just beginning to think about the path Type C is already a wondrous achievement – way to go! (I'd say you were an all-star, but don't want to trigger regression).

The letter "C" has received a bad wrap in the nation since the advent of report cards. It has been unfairly vilified! It has stood for "average", a swear word in our first world. No one in his/her right mind wants to be a SWEAR WORD! And yet, we know that average is the natural place where most people reside. ½ are on one side of it, and ½ on the other.

Consider the last time you were on a seesaw (and I hope it was recently!) Did you sit in the middle by the steel part that holds the wood plank in place while two friends seed and sawed on either side of you? Well, in case you didn't, this is what happens: You would be in the middle – or the average part of the plank. And, with one leg on one side of the steel bar and one on the other, you'd find WHAT??? BALANCE! YES! THE MIDDLE IS WHERE THE BALANCE IS! Type C is VICTORY! And you can achieve it!!

C is, most certainly, <u>not</u> average. C is the sweet spot! It's the place where we can find the most serenity and love and enjoyment and all the other good stuff in this life. It's so pleasant we didn't even need to make a pit stop at Type B on our way. It can fill our hearts without making us crazy. How crazy is THAT?

You can even begin to practice the Type C philosophy as you read this book. Read a few paragraphs and put it down! Take the dog for a stroll! Have a cup of International coffee with a slice of pie. Make it a la mode! Sit for a moment and just listen to yourself breathe.   Like Dorothy in Oz, you've had the power all along, so click your heels together and find your C!

You can be Type C! All it takes is a lot less hard work.

Let your new, carefree life begin!

***Questions To Ponder When Pondering
Your New C Life***

Do you ever wonder why ...

*technology built for convenience tends to make life
more complicated?*

A smart phone doesn't actually make you smarter?

Good to Grateful: How I Drop Kicked My A.

First, I got unemployed. Some might even say sh*t canned. Like many Type As before me, I didn't always realize where my Type A opinion was valued, and where it wasn't. The need for control was too great, as the Type A in me thought it was just about the only way to avoid failure.

So busy was I chasing my own tail at the office, I needed to spend several unemployed weeks, months and years getting my head professionally extricated from up my anal passageway. I attended mental health therapy sessions with the devotion of a born again who only had hours to live. I asked Type A question after question, trying to find the answers.

"What's the point?" I asked the psychologist.

If I couldn't achieve or win something, why did life matter at all? Thankfully, although certainly a difficult head case, I wasn't the first Type A my psychologist had ever seen dent her purple couch.

"Is there an executive program so I can fast track through this?"

I thought my psychologist would understand my need for speed and excellence, as she must be Type A given all of the diplomas on her wall. But alas, she wasn't a Type A any longer, and helped show me the way to sanity.

First, I needed to check my motivation. If I used the word "should", it usually had some Type A meaning tied to it. I began looking at letting things be, as the Beatles instructed, rather than seeing how much I could do. I didn't actually need to constantly prove myself – I was already here!

I soon realized that God is the only one who's wearing a watch with time that matters, and I was forced into freedom for a divine reason! My quest for the C!

I only had to measure up to my standards, and those could be recalibrated to "happy". Success was up to me to determine, and I could make it my next victory or my next peaceful moment!

I must warn you, getting to your C is not for the faint of heart. It is a 24/7 endeavor until you've trained yourself to live a un-scorecarded life. But you CAN do it, and don't even need to get fired (or lose any and/or all worldly possessions) first! You can start right now, or (in true C form) whenever the mood hits you! Just remember: baby steps lead to long, easy strolls.

It took me four, long years to find my C, and (as I had an acute case of it) still have to beat down my A every now and again. But fear not – this book can bring you to balance much quicker (not that is a race, however).

May you find balance, happiness and fulfillment in most everything you do, beginning today!

Whooopeeee!

Do you ever wonder why ...

those who see the glass as half empty usually see it as more empty than that, and those who see the glass as half full filled to the brim?

The Type A Detox

As a Type Cer, I must first point out that everyone gets to detox (and/or extricate) in his or her own free wheeling way. I can only tell you how I did it, hoping that it enables you to find the life you deserve.

Part with Your Smart Phone

I know, I know ... *"You'll have to pry my Blackberry® from my cold, dead hands!!"* But it really doesn't have to be that, well, final. You will not die (I promise) from parting with your PDA! Successful disposal (whether temporary or permanent) is imperative.

If you have anything that rings to remind you of anything short of a baby's feeding, a fire or aliens attacking, it needs to be put to bed every night, and most (if not all) of every day. Consider the following methods of disposal:

If you have a basement:

Buy several pieces of Hotwheels® plastic toy car track. Run it from the top of your stairs to a laundry basket below. Slide the ringy thingy gently down the track into the basket. Repeat until you have all such things out of your hearing range. (Please do NOT set up two tracks to race your Type A spouse to see who can hit the basket first).

If you don't have a basement:

Open a window and simply let it *fly*.

There is no reason on God's good earth that you need to be reachable every second of every minute of every hour of every day! The portable smart things need to recharge, and so do you.

And what's the great thing that happens when you're not available to the boss at the office or can't answer your bizillionth email of the day? You become EMOTIONALLY available to your loved ones! Hugs instead of texts! Story time in place of the 8 pm conference call!

The really crazy part of it is this: When you spend time to recharge your own batteries, you'll do a better job when you actually have to be working or playing! Whooppeee!

A note of caution: Do not, in a fit of panic or irrational or rational thought, try to flush your smart phone down the toilet (unless of course you're at the office, in a hotel, or in someone else's home and your phone is untraceable).

The plumbing costs can be pretty extensive, depending on your level of success. Further, the explanation to your plumber (especially if he doesn't understand the Type C philosophy) can be a bit uncomfortable. He might ask you tough questions such as *"Why didn't you just use the window? Toss it in a trash can? Hand it off to a trusted friend? Try the old Hotwheels® trick?"*

To avoid such uncomfortable questions, use the window. NEVER, under any circumstances, attempt smart phone disposal in an airplane lavatory. a) the flush system makes it nearly impossible for the smart phone to escape and b) if attempted at the beginning of a long flight, you will impede fellow passengers who want to use the lavatory for reasons other than PDA disposal.

Host a Take Out Dinner Party, and Only Invite People You Like

The old you would gourmet chef the heck out of a meal, and invite other Type Aers you want to impress with the feast. The filet would be cooked perfectly or your head would magically blow off, and the vintage wine from your cellar so good it would make the Barefoot Contessa giddy with excitement.

For this dinner party, don't serve anything that doesn't come out of a box, including your vino. Invite people you really like, and who really like you! If this includes other Type Aers, you may be instrumental in their transformation – good for you!

Order dinner from a local take out place (preferably Chinese) and put the white boxes all over your kitchen counter. Ask your guests to serve themselves! If you're feeling really bold, put out the paper plates.

If you're serving fried chicken and mashed potatoes from the Coronel, give attendees their very own sporks to use! And make sure you order the food you enjoy, not simply the stuff that makes you look better in your tankini or swim trunks.

Blast Bob Marley rather than Mozart during dinner, and laugh without shame when you find your spouse has dribbled Egg Fu Young on his t-shirt.

Yes, this party idea will invariably scare the sh*t out of you and your friends, but the flood of emotions it produces will get you further along in your journey. Bon Appétit!

Bring Store Bought Brownies to the Bake Sale.

Go on, you can do it! Leave them in the wrapper, complete with the sticker that lists ingredients and the low, low price you paid, until you arrive at the bake sale. Once there, unwrap the brownies on the table, cut them into uneven squares and place them on a paper plate. Rewrap with saran. Mind you, executing such bake sale blasphemy will no doubt draw a crowd. There might even be some gasps and whispering behind (and in front of) your back. You might feel a sudden sense of shame or guilt, but don't let that own you.

The brownies made by that the nice person at the supermarket are just as delicious as the ones made by your compulsively perfect fellow moms. The only difference is you didn't stay up until midnight baking after running through the Latin for Toddlers flash cards with your two year old and running the infant yoga class in your living room. You read a book. Maybe watched some mind numbing TV after a long day playing with the kids and cuddling with your spouse. Well done!

Show Up On Time for Work

There you are ... in the office parking garage with your hands death gripped to the steering wheel as you wait for the digital clock to read 9:00. No one said this would be easy.

Showing up for work when it is supposed to begin rather than one to two hours prior is an ambitious undertaking. Remain calm. The fear will subside. You might want to take a few practice runs over a weekend or two to get yourself mentally prepared. Dry runs are always a good idea when facing such hurdles.

Visualize the looks you will get from your colleagues when you begin to work on time. This can be very upsetting at the onset. Some might even consider that you're late. A slacker. Uncommitted. You must be ready for their slings and arrows. You know they simply don't have your heightened level of consciousness. Hyperventilation is not uncommon in these situations, so remind yourself to breathe in level measures.

Leave Work at Work

What a novel concept! Let colleagues know, subtly, that you will not answer emails or phone calls or texts or smoke signals once you are home. Tell them a little white lie if need be – you don't have any cell service where you are. Okay, if you live in the middle of New York City in a high rise that will be a more difficult sell, but you get the idea.

Make your home a no work zone for your decompression and the benefit of your family. Gone are the days that you longed for a waterproof Blackberry® so that you could use the minutes you wasted while shaving your face, legs or conditioning your hair. You can enjoy the tranquility of home life with your family, while giving your thumbs and ears and eyes and psyche a much deserved rest.

The Type As will be clawing at the gates, but do not let them enter your sanctuary. Remember, it is a proven fact that people who stress less live longer.

Long live your C-ness!

Throw a Non-themed, No Destination Birthday Party for Your Child

Okay, I know I just made your choke a little. Maybe gasp for breath. Sure, you could be Type C, but how could you endanger the welfare of your child with a birthday party that is not wildly expensive and not damned near logistically impossible to execute?

Little Barbie's mom rented a circus, for God's sake! Spencer's dad didn't settle for just paint ball, he took the 9 year olds to a firing range and gave them live ammo! Then, he hired a real militia so they could *really* play war!

Molly's parents had princess costumes for all of the girls (and even some of the boys) to wear, and hired *real princesses* from a variety of countries as the entertainment! Certainly you have to do SOMETHING that can compete with such efforts.

But alas, NO! Don't do it! Step away from your checkbook and take the party planner off of speed dial. The money spent on your child's birthday party should not equal your share of the national debt. As you tell your children, "just because someone else does it, doesn't make it right."

The child came out of you or your significant other, which gives you oodles of power regarding their lifestyle. Yes, it might be hard for little Johnny to understand, but you can make it a party to remember!

First, tell all invitees that the party will be in your backyard or basement. Decorate said backyard or basement with "Happy Birthday!" messaging from your local low-cost party store. Buy party favors for the kids there, spending no more than $2 per child. Buy a cake at the grocery store, and ask the baker to write "Happy Birthday Johnny!" (or whatever your child's name happens to be) on it in big letters.

At the party, give out noisemakers and party hats and other fun, cheap doo-dads. Play games that require no skill so as not to be Type A competitive and let the kids win nearly worthless but fun prizes.

Serve pizza rolls and potato chips and soda and M&Ms® and all the other fun kid stuff their parents don't consider "brain food." For added excitement, play pin the tail on the donkey with a REAL donkey! (kidding!). Let kids take a baseball bat to the piñata without blindfolds on!

If any child questions the birthday party's theme, tell him/her it's a green theme. Then, send them in the backyard with tools to plant your garden, rake your leaves or till the vegetable patch. If other children want to pitch in, all the better!

If prying parents want to know what you're doing, tell them it's a "Retro Birthday" theme – just like the one you had as a 9-year old kid.   You've decided to bring the kids back to the wonderment and innocence of birthdays of long, long, long ago.

The insecure Type As among them will be mad that they didn't think up such a unique party theme. Hell, they just went the "rent out the paintball arena for 50 kids including several very scared little girls who don't like the idea of being shot" route. What you did was pure genius!

Trying to top the birthday extravaganzas of all of the other Type A parents is not only exhausting, it's impossible! Don't get caught in the trap. Stand out by not doing much of anything at all. Kids innately know how to have fun, you just need to point them in the right direction. A great time will be had by all, you will not freak the hell out of yourself or your spouse, you'll have more money and maybe even a well manicured yard as a result. Happy Birthday to YOU!

Leave Dishes in the Sink

I know what you're thinking, "Whoa! This Type C stuff is great, but I have to draw a line SOMEWHERE!" In some parts of this process, none greater than this one, you're going to have to trust me. Dirty dishes in the sink will free your soul. This is not to say that you get to become a pig or piglet, just less anal about getting everything just right all of the time. Dirty dishes in the sink is symbolic for a life not lived in a never-ending attempt at perfection! Celebrate it! Dance around them with the drying towel you won't be using. Facebook® a photo of the food laden filth and share it with the world! You deserve it!

Consider all of the people who can never, ever leave an unmade bed. Morning after morning, they are compelled to hospital corner the damned thing until you can bounce a brick off of it. And why? Because it would drive them nuts not to. Their Type A has them in a strangle hold, and they can't breathe if they aren't constantly striving for perfection. How exhausting!

If you're a Doubting Thomas or Jane, try the following experiment: Leave dishes in the sink and invite a Type A gal pal over for coffee. Sit or stand in the kitchen while you sip your Folgers®. Make certain she is within eye view of the dishes. Her compulsion is not simply limited to her house! Eventually, given enough time, she will begin to casually clean your dirty dishes.

If you leave her along long enough, beds will magically be made and closets cleaned and book cases dusted. Sadly, she just won't be able to help herself. You could save your own time and/or the cost of a maid service if you were the type to exploit the less fortunate. But as a recovering Type Aer, you can benefit from another's malady.

After all, you're on your merry little way to freedom! You understand purity in moderation! You can keep a neat home, but don't need it to be perfectly neat. You can sleep in, eat bagels and drink inexpensive grocery store bought coffee in bed while you read the paper with your hubby and ponder the things you might feel like doing today – no day planner necessary! Feel your glee filled sigh-exhale, and see the toothy grin on your face. Your dirty dishes can be transformational!

The key to a truly cleansing Type A detox involves slowly removing the anal retentiveness out of your life. Before executing any task (you can use those herein or invent your own!), ask yourself a simple question, "Will the world, as I know it, end if I don't _____ right now or ever?" If the answer is no, go for it! Put the dirty dish in the sink, plug your ears and duck! Did a bomb go off? No! And you're well on your way to achieve a care free existence! Way to go!

Do you ever wonder why ...

calm begins with a C, and Anxiety an A?

people racing through life don't realize it just gets them closer to Kingdom Come?

Don't Jones Over the Jones!

It is imperative that you stop comparing yourself to the other Smiths and Jones. Type Cs celebrate with confidence their own lives and the lives of those around them. If you constantly pull out the measuring stick, you'll never measure up. Why? Because you only see the part of the Type A lives around you that they want you to see. It makes much more sense for your sanity to snap the damned stick in half and focus on your own happiness instead. You're measuring up, too, after all – to you and your life! Well done!

But alas, we are imperfect creatures. There are many times that Type Aers flaunt their riches (feigned and/or factual) in front of our very eyes. And, heck, we're in recovery from A. It's not always easy to turn a blind eye to others overachievements. Let's take, for example, the dreaded Christmas (p.c. "holiday") letter.

Merry Christmas, all!

Frank and the kids and I are very thankful to have had yet another spectacular year! We are truly blessed, as we've surpassed all of our expectations, and our children are damn near perfect!

Jennifer won The Miss America Pageant as a 10 year old, and is going to Dartmouth in the fall. She's torn between solving world hunger or becoming a neurosurgeon while pursuing her career as a model on the runways of Paris. (Knowing her, she'll probably find a way to do all three.) She was also drafted in the third round as a pitcher for the Yankees, but has decided to pursue her education and modeling instead. What a blessing she is!

Jason has really taken to the study of particle physics, and hopes to change the orbit and/or position of the earth in an attempt to solve global warming. Not bad for a 2nd grader! He's also captain of his elementary school glee club, math, lacrosse, soccer, and water polo teams. He's found that he only needs 4 hours of sleep a night, which helps him keep up with the on-line classes he's taking at M.I.T. Our biggest challenge with him is to get his head out of the books at night. Ugh!

My soul mate and best friend and smoking hot lover Frank and I renewed our vows again over Thanksgiving, as we are so thankful for each other every minute of every day! 20 years and two children later and I can still fit into my wedding dress – what a blessing! The photo of the re-nuptials appeared in the wedding section of the New York Times. We had to buy an ad and put the announcement in it, but we thought it was important to share our special moment with the world.

Frank just received yet another promotion at Acme Paper, making him ESVP of Sales and Development and Marketing and Operations and Insights and Strategies for New England! The gigantic bonuses along with his six-figure salary have afforded us some wonderful blessings, and we're very humbled by them. We've traveled the world three and ½ times this year, and plan on hiking the Himalayas without a guide in July.

As for me, I've taken this year to step back and smell the roses. I decided to chair only 4 non-profits, and have cut my other service commitments down to several. Running the charity auction at the country club was taxing but rewarding. We raised over a million dollars by selling adoptable babies from foreign countries. It just goes to show you how generous, kind and welcoming our community is!

Well, I'd better skedaddle. I have to go onto our back 40 to shoot the Christmas turkey.

Thank God for you, dear friends, and for all of our blessings!

Merry Xmas!

With Love,
The Perfectimentes
Mary Frances, Frank, Jennifer, Jason

When you receive a Type A holiday letter, typically with matching sweater picture of the family included, light a fire. Read the letter with only one or no eyes open, then throw it into the flames while singing Elvis' "Burning Love".

They are lying about their perfection or telling the truth. Either way, you don't need to read it. Your life is fine and dandy the way it is, ever changing and filled with imperfection! Celebrate your freedom as their achievements go up in flames!

You might even consider writing your own holiday letter:

Dear Friends,

Happy Holidays!

Love,

(Insert your family name here)

The short form letter will keep the Type As in your life guessing, which is always fun.

Ah, the freedom of not having to be in the horse race. Trot in the fields, graze on the land. Enjoy the C life you so richly deserve. Leave the sprints on the dirt track to those who want to win, knowing that you're winning already!

Do you ever wonder why ...

tombstones don't have spaces to list achievements?

What To Do With Your Type A Child

Is it nature or nurture? Who the Sam Darwin knows! And frankly, only a Type A would obsess about such things. But that aside, you have to play the cards your dealt. You, in your old type A-ness, may have bequeathed Type A onto your child. And, in this day in age, a genetically engineered or culturally formed Type A child is about as common as stars in the clear night sky.

But alas, a reformed you wants have some unscheduled quality time with Junior. Maybe go for ice cream or play catch in the back yard. But he wants to pull out his SAT pop-up book and brush up on his understanding of Plate Tectonics.

You want to visit the playground and climb on the jungle gym. He wants to watch his Yo Yo Ma video for the bizillionth time, mimicking the master's finger movements on the arms of his Lamby.
Although Type C has allowed you to be more comfortable with less than success, you know the dangers of an overachieving life.

At times you may feel like you're pushing an anvil held by a circus fat lady on an elephant uphill, but you know that balance is a journey, not a destination.

Freddy (you used to call him Junior but there's too much pressure in that) might kick and scream, thinking you're endangering his first place holding Teacher's hand in the kindergarten line headed to the natural history museum, but early action on your part will pay dividends (if not Ivy League ones) in the future.

Think of the money you'll save on those damned bumper stickers that brag about little Freddy's achievements at *All Work, No Play Day Care*? You'll be able to look out your rear window without encumbrance from the sea of booster clubs and elite elementary and high school and college decals. You will no longer feel the need to brag about your poor child to complete strangers as you drive merrily down the highway.

Certainly, there are risks involved in lopping off the Type A of your child. All of his/her friends might not have parents such as you, concerned with the delicate balance of a preschooler's psyche. Others might ostracize your child because they view him as bad influence on their child.

How can you invite a child to a structured play date at the pre-Mensa day camp if Freddy has no desire to become one? Your son or daughter may miss the birthday parties themed around Einstein's theory of relativity, and passed over for book clubs involving Shakespeare for the under 6 set. Instead, you can spend the day to kicking it old school with Junior!

On the upside, he will pose no imminent threat to the uber perfectionists among his peers. He might even make it with the ladies, as they'll find him to be dim witted yet charming. He can afford to have a sense of humor and be the life of the 1st grade, because he's not competing for the top in his class.

So what if he doesn't get into the right elementary school which leads to the right high school and the right AP classes and the prestigious private bastion of higher learning? State schools have better football programs! And better tailgate parties! And more to live for on Saturdays than stuffy East Coast institutions.

When was the last time someone drafted a Harvard QB or talked about the hot Princeton cheerleader he dated? Who at Penn knows how to execute a panty raid or construct a fully functional beer bong? The Type C enriched life will offer your son or daughter a myriad of "every man" benefits that Type As can only dream of.
You can really kick some A by raising a C!

Do you ever wonder why ...

we obsess about our age when it really doesn't matter if we're living in the moment?

power and control are sought after by many As to make their lives complete, yet are sterling examples of imbalance?

you can be overwhelmed and underwhelmed but you can't be whelmed?

Getting Passed Over and LOVING It!

It's not that the Type A can't handle getting passed over as much as believe it is something demonic for which there is no acceptance. And, God forbid, when it happens, the screams from the depths of one's soul can be eardrum bursting. Second place? It's the first loser, after all! Who could ever accept that?

But fear not, new Cers – You can!!!! You can smile after the boss makes the absolutely inane choice of Kathy Kissass to head the new team! You won't care that she gets that corner office, the primo parking space or the all office email (with her name in the subject line) that talks about how absolutely wonderful she is.

Because when old Kathy is burning the midnight oil on yet another Friday night, you'll be home with your Type C watching Must See TV on your couch. When she's putting together that presentation for the big client over the weekend, you'll be with your Type C family at the park, enjoying a spring day in the sunshine! Her pasty white skin will not see sun, much like a vampire, and you and your family will dizzy yourself counting each other's freckles.

There will be no missing of another school play for you, no way! You will be front row when your child does a spot on impersonation of a blade of grass. And right before the curtain closes, you might see a harried A parent or 10 running in the back door, attempting to catch their breath and act like they've been there all along. Smile and wave, friends, because you were there all along!

There is the distinct possibility that you may be shunned by Type A friend groups. Type Aers, viewing your quest for balance as some form of laziness, might not pick you for the booster club fundraising committee or ask you to host a stop on the House Walk benefiting the already well endowed private school.

Hold steady, friends! Realize all of the hours you will not have to spend posturing with the alpha dog female on the float building committee about the theme for the 4th of July parade float. Washington crossing the Delaware? Paul Revere's Ride? A Betsy Ross Quilting Bee? Who the hell CARES? Thank your lucky C that you don't have to!

Think of the hours you'll get to spend peacefully on the couch, reading a good book (maybe re-reading even this one!) while others bicker about the right way to fold napkins for the museum gala. You can take a walk, play catch with the dog or even get to know your children! Find other Type Cers and form your own group. Sit around and talk about your lives honestly. Nothing says balance like good conversation over coffee and store bought brownies.

Yes, getting passed over does take some getting used to, but it is okay. In the end, you'll be passing through life rather than racing it until it passes you by.

Do you ever wonder why ...

they call it a deadline?

What to do when you find you're pushing up to a C+/B-

STOP! Get control of yourself! You don't really want to go back to a place where you'd trip your ailing grandmother on the way to the "All you wouldn't eat because of caloric content Buffet" just to say you got there first.

Consider the following diversions:

Pharmaceuticals!
Get a trusted doctor to give you a little something for the anxiety and potential depression resulting from the loss of your Type A life. Mind you, this is only a short-term solution. Drugging yourself into a Type C state is not advised.

Therapy!
Talk to a trained someone about the loss of your Type A life. (Try to make sure the therapist is not a Type A, as that might really and truly screw with your head.) You'll be amazed all of the places your Type A sticks out, from getting the best parking spot at the grocery store to training to summit the backside of Everest. A good therapist will be able to point out all of ways you A, and help you find your inner C.

Pointless Exercise!
No, not the kind that involves medals, but the kind
that allows you to breathe fresh air and feel the
sunshine on your face! Get your heart rate up,
release those endorphins, and calm the heck down!
If you receive a t-shirt, trophy, or medal – if there is a
start or a finish line or if there is an umpire or referee
or if anyone is keeping score, it is NOT pointless. If
you are keeping score, it's really not pointless! Take
off the heart rate monitor, turn off the calorie burn
measurer, and lose the bib number.   Let yourself
loose to sweat and pant all on your own.

Type C Fellowship!
Have your C friends on speed dial. Go for lunch at a
non-chain diner or meet in someone's kitchen. Tell
them about your concerns, and let them talk you off
the ledge!

Remember, getting to a Type C personality is not an
easy journey for Type Aers. It takes a boat load of
hard work to become laid back. To find balance. To
be able to sit on a beach and not lunge for the cell
when it chirps or tweets or vibrates. You need to
rely on others to help you find your way to balance.
But it is, most certainly, worth it.

Type Aers don't smell the coffee, for goodness sake, as much as they simply ingest it for energy. You have the power within you to pick flowers and hug trees, take quiet walks at night, stare at the stars and ponder life in its fullest. Don't slip back into the abyss of rank, achievement and productivity! You're much more valuable than that.

If you really feel that you're falling down the A hole, do this little exercise: count your blessings. No, really! Write 'em down and count them. And don't do it like an A, but a C. Thank the universe for the pizza delivery man, for self cleaning ovens, for your kid's artwork on the refrigerator, for the Sunday morning crossword, for swing sets and birds and rainy days and sunny ones and time to read and walks and anything else you can think of – the smallest to the largest! I guarantee your hand will tire before you're out of things to add to the list.

And when you're done with your blessings list, put it up on the refrigerator. Add to it as needed. It'll remind you what your life is about when the A gets a temporary hold of your brain.

Did you ever notice ...

the human body was built with two of just about everything to give us balance?

If Life Gives You Lemons, You Have Lemons!

One thing Type Aers are not so great at is accepting life on life's terms.

But here's the terrific news: You're only accepting "defeat" if you consider it defeat!!!

Yeeee haaaa!

Sometimes things are just not meant to be. Most of life is out of our control, whether we want to admit it or not. So, we can either let it eat us alive, or we can try to fix only the fixable things in our lives. We can pick and choose our priorities without calling them "battles." By letting go of the host of things that you cannot control, you will actually gain more control and balance in your life. I know it sounds crazy, but it really works!

The next time you're stuck in traffic, don't be pissed off and consider the untimely deaths of fellow motorists by your own two hands or the bug laden grill of your car. Instead, realize that you can't change the circumstance and BREATHE. Forces beyond your control have put you in that traffic jam, and you can either curse it or fill your mind with other more fruitful thoughts like what's for dinner or why dogs are the only animals to have their own "years." Dog years? Hmmm. But I digress.

When the person who was behind you in line tries to become the pushy person ahead of you, consider the circumstance and then react! Boarding an airplane? Heck, it won't take off without you, right? Is it in the grocery store? (Well, in that case, nail 'em! No one would should get to diss you in the shopping check out line.)

We all have our limits, don't we? Simply set your boundaries and decide how you feel about any circumstance. If it feels bad, take action! Being a C doesn't mean you're a patsy! You have every right to a beautiful life, and cannot accept the bullying of As. Stand up, Cs! Stand up!

Type Cers accept their circumstances as best they can and move on. We are not slackers. We are not lazy. We are not victims! No say we! We are Zen like beings committed to living the life we were meant to live the way were meant to live it! Halleluiah!

So when life gives you lemons, you get to decide what to do with 'em! Lemonade? Lemon Meringue pie? Or just plain lemon for your ice water. Drink it up!

Did you ever notice that ...

People who say "money can't buy you happiness" are usually the ones who have tried it?

New Moms: Live in Fear-less-ness!

The number one fear of every new mother I've ever
met is that she will somehow screw up her child or
(in the case of multiple births) children. The
intersection of Type A and child rearing is the most
frenetic and chaotic and stress filled place in this
world! There is no perfection in a dirty diaper or a
snot filled nose or the ear infection that comes and
goes with the tides. Yet, in hopes of finding
perfecting, we cheer the little guy like he's just
closed a multi-million dollar merger when he finally
gets the hang of the potty. And we completely freak
out if she's not speaking in full sentences moments
after exiting the womb.

Type A Society tells young moms that they have to
read every book, buy every educational toy, speak to
their children in very specific ways, look for clues
24/7 about the child's development, feed them the
perfect foods – the list goes on and on.

Doing everything "right" is one thing – IMPOSSIBLE!
Type C gives you permission to stop beating yourself
up and exhale! Your mom didn't have nearly as
much pressure to raise the perfect child as you do,
and look how you turned out.

You're aware, concerned, maybe even a little frantic but very present. Your kids will learn great things from you, even when you feel you've made mistakes. Mom is WOW upside down – and a switch from A to C will only help your relationship with your children.

Moms have to accept that young children reek of wonderful imperfection! What was a beautifully appointed home with everything in its rightful place looks like a megaton bomb hit it, and will for the next several years. This is what made the ingestion of Xanax and Chardonnay (sometimes simultaneously) so danged popular with the Type A mom! When perfection is the goal and chaos is the reality, the A psyche simply can't handle it.

But here is the soothing salve for concerned moms, Type A or otherwise – you will not ruin your kids!!! They will still be your kids when the house is messy, when you skip a play date or two to get some "me" time, when the world seems just a little bit upside down. Open the door and toss the Tiger Mom book or any other "this is the only way to rear a perfect child" book out the damned door and go with your heart! Accept that perfection is impossible.

Heck, my generation didn't even have seat belts in the car, let alone car seats and baby monitors and child rearing books and infant educational videos and bike helmets and play dates and other such things, and most of us are still around! After the first five kids my mom barely noticed when I jumped out of the birth canal, but some would say I turned out all right!

Young Type A mothers, the Type C approach will set you free. You're doing it right whatever way your heart tells you to do it! Way to go!

Did you ever notice ...

Type A is so Type A it has the first letter of the alphabet?

Achieve the Wants, Not the Have Tos, in Your Life

If you need to do something to reach a want, go for it. But if you need to do something to reach something you think you have to or should do, hold your horsies!

You're no slacker as a C, you have simply balanced the scales in your life. This doesn't mean you won't want to achieve things, or have success in your life – far from it! But the Type C philosophy will help you realize what you really want rather than running towards things you think you're supposed to achieve. Life is soooo much more fun than that!

Take the academic bastion of the Type A, the MBA. It's about as common as clowns at a carnival these days. But, alas, you were told you must have one to climb, claw or dig your way up the corporate ladder. Yet, if everyone on your block has a bicycle, getting one too is really no big woop, is it?

It took years to attain the status, and boatloads of money and sacrifice. For what? To get a level or two further up the food chain? Is there some secret of life that will help you live more richly or longer that you learned putting the M next to your BA? Maybe you have had such an epiphany – good for you! Or maybe you did it to keep up with everyone else around you. Ouchy!

The Type C approach will lead you away from A traps, leaving you with more time, money and piece of mind. You don't have to follow the path of all of those around you to achieve happiness! Blaze your own trail! Ray Kroc never went to college! Sam Walton never chaired a bake sale! If you feel you want to learn more or do more of anything for the right reasons, go for it. But if you're just doing it to get somewhere else or doing it simply for achievement's sake, reconsider.

Like anything in life, check your motivation. Will X, Y, Z make your life better? Make you happier? Give you more moments of joy? More freedom? That, my friend, should be your litmus test. Do what you need to do only if it gets you closer to having the life you want.

Remember, there's no A in joy, and there's a big C in CHOICE! Trust your heart and let your life fly, without regret, shame or time wasted doing sh*t you don't care about!

Did you ever wonder why ...

*If someone hurts you personally its considered cruel,
but if they do it at the office "it's just business?"*

If You're Considering a Work/Life Balance, You're Already in Deep Doo-Doo

Merely pondering such a work/life balance shows your Type A is struggling to do it all, to be all the things your achieving Type A self can be! The vast majority of persons contemplating work/life balance are not living more life, but working more work. It should be renamed, "How do I extricate my hind end out of my chair at the office without putting my A in a tizzy and jeopardizing whatever that magical something is that I'm attempting to achieve at the office so I get on with some kind of life?" No one on his/her deathbed ever says, "Gosh, I wish I had spent more time at work!" Set your C boundaries!

Work as much as is necessary, not unnecessary. The Daughters of the American Sisterhood's Revolutionary Ball, PTA chairpersonship, Private School fundraisers and all other competitive environments don't need to rule your life. You are the master or mistress of your destiny! Exercise your freedom! Do the one person march right out the door when the whistle blows, and go home to see those kids you made and hang out with that spouse or dog or house plants that give your life purpose.

Your Life balance requires, in most cases, the need for work. Work you hopefully really enjoy. But it is still work. And A's are known workaholics.

You've never heard of a lifeaholic, have you?

Because we Cs keep that under wraps, so as not to seem competitive with others. And addiction to the life we live rather than the work we do is key to the C! So push back from the table and head for home. You deserve it!

Do you ever wonder why ...

People who say they "won't settle for second best"
are never satisfied?

The A-ddiction to Competition

Okay, let's be honest here. Competition for Aers is like black tar heroin to a junkie. I, for one, LOOOVED it. Any form! Marathons, ideas at the office, lines in the grocery store, parking spots, thumb typed words per minute – you name it. Type As have an innate need to strive for superiority. Even if we don't mean to. It's the "est" in our lives. Best. Most. We fly over one hurdle and set our sights on the next. It's just the way the A has been since cave man time.

The invention of the wheel didn't happen by accident. Caveman A was pissed off that some other guy created fire and he wanted to bury him for it. And so the term "bested" came about. It all goes back to the cavemen. Who's the best hunter gatherer? Who looks best in a saber tooth tiger skin? Who has the biggest cave? Best cave art? We've been at this since the dawn of mankind, so cut yourself some slack. It might take awhile to go from A to B to C.

The following fact might help you along in your battle against competition: If you do anything simply to win, you're already losing. Don't set goals just because you don't know what else to do with your free time. Have free time, instead!

And yes, it might sound simple in theory and be a b*tch to execute, but you can do it! You're smart enough (don't need to be the smart"est") after all! Surely you can figure out how to take the race out of your run.

Experiment with activities that, on the surface, you can't win. Even though you might think there's a possible competitive angle, you can't win yoga. Believe me, I tried. The concept that there's no wrong way to do it blew my mind. I hated it at first, much like I hated aerobics in the 80s. Only I hated yoga more because I was supposed to be relaxed by it.

I was so inflexible and so stressed about my performance my first yoga instructor corrected my breathing before we moved into the first pose. My breathing! Sh*t, I couldn't even get that right. After several weeks and a few wines before an evening class, I realized I couldn't win. Simply being there was enough.

Then there was the marathon, my 15th, that I ran "just for fun." Obviously, I was working out some of the kinks in my C strategy at the time, as running a marathon is A no matter what way you slice it, but I digress.

I didn't wear my Ironman stop watch, which I would gaze upon each mile, knowing that towards the end of 26.2 of them I was so delirious I wouldn't understand what the numbers meant anyway. It was just as painful as all the rest, but only longer. The difference? I let myself enjoy it as much as you can enjoy such things. I greeting the crowds, kissed a few babies, and shared positive affirmations with my fellow runners. Whooppee!

Run Free! Take it Easy! You Deserve It!

Do you ever wonder why ...

It's called an "undergraduate degree", but you actually graduate?

Drawing Chalk Outlines Of Your Own Body By Your Desk (so that your colleagues know you're gone).

Often when you've lived and breathed in a Type A work environment, it is wildly difficult for colleagues to figure out A, you're not an A anymore and B, vacation means vacation. It comes from the Latin vacante (okay, I made that up). It means gone. Absent. No longer there.

But, alas, your Type A teammates might not get that memo. They'll want to call you on your vacation, while in the hospital delivering a baby or as you lay dreamingly on a beach wondering why it is you work at all.

After you set your away messages on the email and the office phone and the cell and finish skywriting your departure above corporate headquarters, take time to draw a chalk outline of your own body at your desk. Simply lay down with side walk chalk and begin to trace. If you're holding a briefcase, all the more believable! When you've finished, cordon off the area with yellow police tape.

Those who didn't listen to your away messages or see the skywriting will think you're dead, which will work to your advantage. Even Aers don't typically attempt to wake the dead.

You'll get the peace and quiet you richly deserve, and people will say really nice things about you while you're (temporarily) gone. And coming back from the dead will really impress your colleagues.

Aloha!

Do you ever wonder why …

Lawyers and Doctors practice, and the rest of us work?

Taking the FU out of FUN

Having "fun" with Type As is often an oxymoron. A's enter wildly competitive and/or extreme events and disguise them as "play." (Note: anything you can die from is not play.) Type A's often "relax" with the aid of adult beverages. (In a Type C's book, that's cheating). And often, given no alcohol or no competition, Type As just don't know how to completely have fun. I like to call it the Type A FU. Without the n, it's simply not fun.

When leaving your Type Aness, it might be hard at first to see when you're not having fun. The following indicators and suggestions will help you along the way:

If you find yourself on top of your Great Aunt Betty in the back yard as she's screaming "Uncle!", you're not having fun. Racing others on the jogging path, trying to bury your own kids in a game of Monopoly®, betting on which elevator will come first are all signs of A-ness and should be avoided at all costs. They're simply un-fun!

If you are keeping score, keeping track, or in any way/shape/form measuring yourself against the abilities of others, it's not play.

un is the only 3-letter word that describes
ntertaining play. Having "fun" beats the heck out
 f having "fu", and will lower your stress level and up
your joy every time.

One of the biggest mistakes As make is that they
think they grow out of fun. You're never to old to
play on the swing set or climb a tree or eat a two
decker ice cream cone. C's do crazy stuff like that all
the time!

So, put the book down for a second and have some
F-U-N! Your inner child will thank you for it!

Do you ever wonder why ...

Some people would rather talk about how busy they are than how they feel?

The Inherent Dangers of Type As Running the World

Letting Type As think they run the world is like letting men think they run the house. What harm does it do, provided you're still the one holding onto the reins? The biggest danger known to man is when the wrong Type As really do run the show.

I'm guessing that Jesus, Vishnu, Allah, Yahweh, the Dalai Lama and any other deity you'd like to throw in the hopper were not Type As. Far from it. They are actually Type Cs in leadership positions. Jesus preached peace, after all, not aggression. He didn't start a war. He didn't try to compete with his fellow man. He didn't try to run an empire or get the biggest shack in the village or fastest donkey cart in town.

Sure, God did do that little flood that wiped out everyone but Noah and his animal pals, but He also gave us Job, the man that lost everything but kept his faith. Very Type C of him. And the Type A Cain was a lesson of whom not to be, as his aggressiveness lead to the untimely death of his brother, Abel.

I remember, as a Type A, thinking the Dalai Lama was adorably cute and well meaning, but thought he must have been dropped on his head as a child. How else could you explain his calm demeanor? He seemed to need nothing other than peace and a saffron robe or two, and yet he was always smiling! What was up with THAT?

Surely you can't be that damned happy moving that slow. You never see clips of him running through an airport to catch an earlier flight or trying to find his way to the head of any line. He doesn't raise his voice or curse or throw tantrums or try to take over companies or belittle any of his fellow men and women for personal or professional gain. And yet, millions around the world love and respect him. He's the essence of Type C, a leader who doesn't need to push to bring people along with him for the ride.

Without argument, the biggest human tragedies are caused by Type As in leadership positions. Could you see Jesus as General of an Invading Army? Vishnu a corrupt, self-serving politician? Would Yahweh ever have become Bernie Madoff? Not a chance. They wouldn't take advantage of others for his own selfish gains. Power and greed and hate are not the tools of the C.

Personal peace of any kind is not a concept that lots of Type As can understand. When achievement is a constant and solitary way you consider how you measure up, then peacefulness might make you believe you're not trying hard enough. Just being is the opposite of doing, and therein lies the rub. Everyone needs peace to live a long, healthy and fulfilled life.

Take, for example, the Sea Turtle. Provided it doesn't get eaten by some food chainer, it will live over a hundred years. It is the mellowest of all beings, quietly gliding about the water eating vegan specialties served up by mother nature. And talk about calm! If we all breathed like Sea Turtles, we would live well past historic averages.

All of us can achieve monumental things in our lifetimes. It all depends on how you measure success. Is it outdoing the Jones, or living a life filled with joy? Living foot loose and fancy free? The secret is finding your sweet spot. Your balance. Jumping off the damned treadmill and taking life on your terms and at your pace with your heart in mind.

When you feel you've lost your way and get caught in the magnetic pull of the Type A, remember the Sea Turtle. Quietly wave your flipper and GLIDE.

Do you ever wonder why ...

Nice guys finish last? Or who is actually doing the judging? With what yard stick?

Don't Go to D

Just as you should avoid the driven, obsessive, race you to Hell to get there first attitudes of an A (or possibly a B), you must avoid the pull of the D (and God forbid the F) at all costs. Going from an achievement-aholic to a tree sloth is neither good for you or those who share your air space. You're looking for the middle ground here, not a deep, dark black hole.

As the pendulum swings from Aer back to balance, it may whiz past the C and land you in the D. This is to be expected, but you must be mindful of the threat and potentially unpleasant consequences. Going from "I have to be 15 minutes early to get the best spot in the kid pick up line at the elementary school" to "hell, they know how to call a cab" is not living in the C. Nor is a lack of hygiene, giving car keys to someone under the age of 16 to hit the drive-thru or eating more than one meal in a row in bed (unless, of course, you're seriously ill).

It makes sense that, after years of being wound tighter than a drum, your newfound peace might ooze out all over the place. Unmonitored, you might gain a few pounds, grow a goatee and bury any and all alarm clocks under the dirty laundry in the closet. For God's sake, get a hold of yourself! Remember the freaking see saw! You must find the middle of things!

Seek out your emotional symmetry. Put yourself squarely between the ying and the yang of things. Be the C in CHE. Some days you'll have to be more C+, some days more C-. The goal here is to average the C. On days when your responsibilities drive you a bit more, rise to the occasion. You can get things accomplished without losing your C. On days that you have less on the to do list, give your self additional time to sit and enjoy the view!

Balancing is an act. *Balance* is a blessing!

Do you ever wonder why ...

Those who wish there were more hours in the day wouldn't use them for play?

A in Disguise

There is nothing more dangerous than a Type A in full camouflage. You'll find them lurking at company picnics and block parties, acting like the three-legged race is just for fun. They'll be the ones in the office that seem uninterested in success, but manage to grease every rung you're supposed to climb on the corporate ladder. They will be the pious ones who cut you off in the church parking lot with a wave, and the ones who knock the popcorn out of your hands on the way the best seats in the movie theater. Yes, we've all been them once or twice or a gazillion times before.

They are a stealth and tricky breed of A, and must be approached and engaged with caution. A true Type C won't look to defeat them, but simply outmaneuver them. If you end up moving ahead as a byproduct of the process, so be it. Keeping yourself out of harms way should be your first concern. Type Cs are not doormats, after all, and at times we need to protect our balance.

But here's a secret – Cs always have the upper hand. Consider the fine sport of log rolling. Who ends up in the drink every time? The one who is off balance!

The one who becomes most aggressive at the worst possible time, leaving the door open for the twinkle toed Cer at the other end of the log who is committed to his/her balance. As a C, you will have the power in your hands (or feet, of course, if you're log rolling).

You can often catch Aers off balance because of their "look for the finish line and/or any other signs of victory) focus. Cs are engaged in the process. Cs stand directly over their feet, living in the present rather than focusing on any particular outcome. By looking too far off into the distance, a C can catch an A unaware. Mind you, the A's hyper vigilance makes them quick to catch on, so your window of opportunity might be minimal.

One of the more dangerous places to discover As is in the exit row seating of an aircraft. They're there because, most likely, they didn't get their upgrade to 1st class and they're probably a little pissed about it. (Frequent flyers get the first dibs at exit row because it has more leg room and they travel too much, not because of benevolence).

When seating in the exit row, the flight attendant will ask if you, in the event of an emergency, are willing and able to open the emergency door. You must say yes, or asked to be moved. (The same flight attendant will serve you adult beverages while you're sitting in the exit row, and we're not supposed to think that might affect one's abilities to carry out his/her duties, but I digress.)

So let's say you are in the middle of that "unlikely event" they always talk about over the loud speaker during the pre-flight instructions. After the plane comes to an abrupt and unscheduled halt, who do you want to be in command of the emergency door? Yep, a C. Why? You can be damned sure those As will get the door off its hinges. The challenge might be if they stick around to pull anyone else out with them.

Certainly there are people the As need to call on their smart phones to say they'll be late. Then there are the emails they'll have to send to reschedule meetings, the calls to book a limo to take them from the crash site, etc. There simply might not be time for the As to help the other poor bastards off the plane, and no one really knows if it will explode, anyway! Jet fuel pouring out of the side of an aircraft does not a fire necessarily make, after all.

And yes, there are As who would help others off the plane, and God willing they're in the exit rows. If an A is behind you in line to get off of that plane, however, be on guard. Carrying all of the things you're supposed to leave behind, the aggressive A is now armed with what could and may very well be used as deadly weapons. A briefcase to the groin to get off first is fair game. A roller bag coming out of the overhead onto your noggin would be enough to stun and/or cripple, thus creating a passing lane. Elbows may be thrown, and you might end up in the crotch of some old fat man with a seat belt extender who couldn't reach the buckle to extricate himself.

In the event of an emergency, there's no time to consider teaching any life lessons to the A. Get your butt off of the plane ASAP, helping whomever you can along the way if at all possible. If not, get your butt off of the plane and look to see if others around you need assistance. (It's great to live the C life, but there's no such thing as a dead C. You're just plain dead.)

Thankfully for the world's sake, most As are overt. They can't hide their A-ness no matter how hard they try. Eventually, it spews out for the entire world to see. Many As, like the former me, live in a place of A-denial. In my twenties, I thought I was laid back and cool. Once I hit 30 I realized I was up tight, hell bent and all about the next hurdle I needed to clear. Thank God for my 40s!

We all have As in our life (including of present or former selves) whom we love and care immensely for. Keep in mind that the A might not see any problem in being an A, or might not even consider him/herself in the A category. But alas, actions don't lie. All Cs can do is set our own lovely boundaries and try to help our As stay within theirs.

Do you ever wonder why ...

Most people don't realize that living in the present is one?

The Good Old Days

There are those of us lucky enough to remember a time of manual car windows. The kind you actually had to roll all the way down, and all the way up. The car radio that had little buttons you had to press in to make the radio change stations. Garage doors that you had to raise yourself. Games that didn't require TV sets or electrical outlets.

We remember TVs that didn't have more than 8 channels, and didn't come with remote controls. When phones were only in a home or office, and you could only carry them as far as the cord would allow. There was life before the internet and personal computers and cell phones and smart phones. Imagine that!

There was a time when one could only be reached by home or office phone or by mail. And if the phone line was busy, you had to wait until it wasn't to reach out and touch someone. We didn't text our friends, but stopped by to say hello. We didn't have our own phones, but shared one with a house filled with other people. And life was a lot less stressful, and a lot less A.

Technology is certainly a double-edged, razor sharp sword. It can make our lives easier on the surface, and much more complicated underneath it. Try to explain to a young person today the concept of writing a letter and having it take three days to get to the recipient. Then, waiting a week or two for the response. That would seem like insanity! But it taught us to be patient.

We didn't play video games. Instead, we played outside. A host of mental and medical issues simply didn't exist before we became so tech savvy. We were closer to the C 50 years ago, and we didn't even know it!

Things that are supposed to make our lives easier often make them more complicated. When someone sends an email, he/she expects an immediate response. If you don't answer your cell phone at all hours of the day or night, the boss might think you're a slacker. But this simply isn't so! We can change the tides of technology by using it to our advantage.

C stands for Control. We can control our lives rather than having our lives control us. We can use innovations to suit our needs, rather than letting them run us into the ground.

At the height of my A years, I prayed for a waterproof Blackberry® so that I could work in the shower so that I could get a jump on the 100 plus work emails I got in a day. How warped is that? I no longer stress about getting back to people the second or minute or hour or day they contact me. Instead, I let them think I'm a little flighty.

Home with the kids? Kick it old school! Turn off the video games and make the kids go outside. Tell them it's "reality play!" Stop the texts and have a conversation! Get off the internet and explore the world around you! Read a book or a newspaper rather than the alerts sent to our PDAs.

Technology is making us more A than we were meant to be. So, make good new days by bringing back the old ones!

Set down all hand held devices, put your hands over your head and wave to the Universe, proclaiming your freedom! Yahhoooo!

Do you ever wonder why ...

Strangers are nicer inside a store than they are on a crowded sidewalk?

Type C Rules of the Road

For some, including me, the hardest thing to drop in my A was how I behaved in traffic. It took months of thoughtful prayer and meditation, but it was not easy...

The middle finger is not a directional signal. Okay, maybe it is but NOT one that C's use unless it is accompanied by the other digits while executing a kind wave or giving permission to another motorist to enter into one's lane.

Even for the best intentioned of us, the A can grab the steering wheel with its titanium talons and drive us to the precipice of hell.

When you find yourself behind the wheel and behind an A-hole or in front of one or if you're the one, take a deep breath in. And out. And in. And out. Like a sea turtle. They live longer than any other thing on the planet because of their serenity.

Put down any and all caffeine you might be ingesting. (I won't suggest you hang up the phone or stop texting, because you shouldn't be doing that anyway.)

Find the classical station or better yet one that only plays bubble gum music from the 70s. Heck, if they sang about Armageddon in the 70s it would be up tempo.   Lord knows it's hard to sing *"Boogie Wonderland"* while eating a crabby pants sandwich.

If weather permits (i.e., you're not in a typhoon, being invaded by locusts or witnessing the Chariots of Fire coming from on High), roll down your windows. In full operatic voice, belt out whatever song or commercial jingle or traffic report is coming out of the speakers. Smile a toothy grin on your inhales.   This will completely disarm the type As in your midst, and most likely scare the sh*t out of any passengers you might have in your automobile. But alas, it is better than the alternative and does have its rewards.

Fellow motorists will think that you're one crazy mother f-er. The crossing guard at the elementary school will wave you into primo handicapped parking area while you wait to pick up your kids. People in the grocery store parking lot, motivated by authentic fear, will park as far away from you as humanly possible. Jackasses in the traffic jam with you won't be so quick to cut you off, fearing you might use your auto as a weapon or, worse yet, you might be packing. (Note: it is not suggested that you execute any of the above in view of any members of law enforcement for reasons I think are pretty darn obvious).

When you feel that you're back in a semi-balanced emotional state, turn down the music, your voice and roll up the windows. With the hand not on the wheel, pat yourself on the back! You deserve it!

You've realized, even if you didn't realize it, that it's only driving. It's only time. Getting mad and darting through traffic like Mario Andretti only accelerates your stress level, and for what? A few extra minutes?

If you find yourself unable to find your inner C, pull safely over to the side of the road, put on your hazards and turn off the car. Point the rear view mirror at your face and repeat these precious words:

"I'll be a few minutes late."

Once you have mastered it in a calm and believable tone, reach for your cell phone. Call whomever is going to notice you'll be arriving slightly behind schedule. Say the words and hang up. Now wasn't that easy???? (If no one will notice your tardiness, simply omit the use of the cell phone and talk to yourself in a soothing yet confident tone.)

After years of experience, I can promise you that getting mad at traffic won't make it go away. Flipping off a fellow motorist who resembles the back end of a horse will not make either of you better persons.

Your new-found Type C driving habits will help you live a longer, less stressed life. Don't worry about five minutes here or there – you're going to outlive the bastard who just cut you off. How awesome is THAT?

You need not rule the roads, but overcome them!

Happy Trails!

Do you ever wonder why ...

You might have dozens of seats in your home, but can only sit in one at once?

Living Green Tips for Your old Type A Life

Recycle Your Smart Phones for Charity!

If you're like I was, you might have more than one PDA or cell phone. Maybe even three. Or four. And yet, you should only be able to have one real conversation at a time.

But there's a way you can rid yourself of your gadgets and raise money for charity (yours or someone else's) at the same time! All you need is a high pedestrian traffic area and a hammer. Lay your phones on a table (or the ground) and let strangers take 3 whacks at them for a buck! There's enough hidden rage, tension and hatred around the smart phone to make lots of cash.

(Alternate executions: PDA Garden Gnomes, Smart Phone Wind Chimes)

Rainy Day? Do Day Planner Decoupage!

Do you really need to schedule every second of every minute of every waking hour of your life? Heck no! Get out that Day Planner and go to town!

Uncarefully rip every last page out of the book. (If it has a metal binder, do not engage the mechanism — rip away instead! Much more cathartic!) Keep ripping until you have lots of little, manageable pieces.

You might find this particular exercise particularly difficult. If you need to get liquor-ed up, so be it! Just remember to stay away from any/all sharp objects if Johnny Walker is in the house.

Dip the pieces in a sticky goo of your choosing, and you're ready to decoupage!

Decorate ornaments, coffee tables, and wall hangings — even your best china! There's no limit to your artistic abilities, and no right or wrong way to do it. Knock yourself out!

(Alternate executions: Day planner confetti, packing material, paper airplanes, shooting range targets.)

Do you ever wonder why ....

The Dalai Lama is always smiling?

The "Correct" Approach

Rarely will you find a Type A who stops at simply attempting to perfect his/her own life. The magnetic pull of perfection is simply too powerful, and oozes out of the very pores of an A. When you achieve C, you get to release your own need for the impossible, *and* the demands you place on others! How cool is THAT?

It is, however, a hard habit to break. But you can do it! When you're in line at the store and you see that the woman in front of you has the tag showing from the back of her sweater *I implore you*, DO NOT TUCK IT IN. Fight the urge! The fact that the name of the apparel manufacturer is protruding from the back of her ensemble is neither life threatening nor your problem! You're a C – A balanced individual who understands boundaries! Yippee yahoo for you!

Obsessively correcting others' grammar (short of your own children) or finishing their sentences (especially with words they wouldn't choose or might not even know) are big time no-nos. You would not like such things to be done to you, so why do this to someone else? Be free in your C, and you'll be able to leave their Ps and Qs alone!

Thoughts of religion or politics and or controversial topics of any sort need not become a death match! As a C, you don't need to prove your correctness and/or superiority to the world! And why? Because it simply doesn't matter! You're free of having to be right all of the time, knowing that it is statistically impossible! You can let others have their opinions without feeling the need to right their ship. Whoopeee!

Lectures of any sort are off limits for the C unless, of course, you're a paid member of academia, the clergy, or a talk show host in front of a willing audience. Telling others how to think, feel or act typically doesn't go over well to the recipient of your certainly stellar advisement. If your opinion is asked for, feel free to deliver it in a judicious and sensible matter.

Conversation rather than conversion to your way of thinking is sweet nectar to the soul, and you will find the love and acceptance of friends and strangers more readily available because of your newfound sense of balance!

Further, you need not be lectured to by others, no matter how well intentioned. Redirect the conversation or simply leave it! If you mother, for example, couldn't make you perfect with her pearls of wisdom in the 18 years or so when she had your undivided attention, why would you think her lectures could save you now? Politely tell your loving mom that you understand and appreciate her opinions, but your hair suddenly caught on fire and you must hang up the phone before the smoke alarms get wind of it. Ah, the sweet smell of burning hair and freedom!!!

Praise the deity of your choosing!!!

Do you ever wonder why ...

People who age are considered over some non-existent hill?

Still not sure where you stand?
Take the Type A Quiz!

Do you (or someone you happen to know) ....

Wear full make-up to attend an aerobics class or a 10K race? Waterproof to swim?

Have a Day Planner for the kids broken up into 5 minute increments?

Make the hotel room bed instead of leaving it for the maid?

Iron your jeans?

Have a statue of Martha Stewart, surrounded by candles, in lieu of the Virgin Mary, Buddha, Vishnu or a crucifix?

Use a magnifying glass, protractor and/or GPS to find the perfect position for fresh cut flowers (from the garden, of course!) on the dining room table?

Make a cell phone call in a public bathroom and wait for someone else's flushing sound to abate before continuing where you left off?

Try to win at Pilates? Yoga? Meditation class?

Secretly believe people who aren't Type As like you are simply not as smart or driven?

Put coasters under complete strangers' drinks at parties?

Give thumbs a nightly ice bath after frolicking all day on the PDA?

Buy 100 boxes of daughter's Girl Scout Cookies so your daughter will be the top seller in her troop?

Have your SAT score tattooed on a portion of your buttocks?

If you answered "yes" to one or more of these questions, there's a damned fine chance you (or someone you know) is an A.

As a C we know that freedom is in being, not in doing. Rejoice in yourself and let the shi-hay hit the fan! It will anyway, and if you're a C you'll know how to position yourself out of harm's (and the fan's) way!

Do you ever wonder why ...

we're here in the first place?

Welcome to the beginning of your Type C Life!

Made in the USA
Monee, IL
09 January 2022

88532061R00059